Except for Figure 5, all the objects and old photographs are from the collection of the author. The paintings beginning with Figure 45 are the work of the author.

Made of Thunder, Made of Glass: American Indian Beadwork of the Northeast is published by Gerry Biron in conjunction with an exhibition of the same title organized by the Abbe Museum in Bar Harbor, Maine. The exhibition will be on view from May 25, 2006 through November 18, 2006 and a second exhibition will be held at the Memorial Hall Museum in Deerfield, Massachusetts from May 1, 2007 through October 31, 2007.

ISBN 9 780978 541408

Published by:
Gerry Biron
PO Box 250
Saxtons River, Vermont 05154-0250

2006

Abbe Museum, Bar Harbor, Maine. Photo by Peter Travers, courtesy of the Abbe Museum.

The Gerry Biron Collection was exhibited for the first time at the Abbe Museum, Bar Harbor, Maine, from May 25 through November 18, 2006. In addition to Mr. Biron's beadwork collection, the exhibit includes selections from Mr. Biron's collection of historical photographs of Native people, including beadworkers, and of non-Native people wearing or displaying beadwork they have acquired from Native artists. Mr. Biron also generously loaned to the exhibition eleven portraits he has painted of Native people, based on historic photographs. In these paintings the artist has incorporated beadwork from his collection.

Special thanks to:

- Gerry Biron for the generous loan of his collection, art, research, support, his essay and this publication.
- Special Friends of the Abbe whose generous support made this exhibit possible.

The mission of the Abbe Museum is to further the understanding and appreciation of Maine's Native American cultures, history and archaeology. The Museum's exhibitions and programs focus on the Native American tradition in Maine and explore the broader Native American experience, past and present.

Made of Thunder, Made of Glass: Niagara Falls and Its Influence on the Production of American Indian Beadwork of the Northeast

by Gerry Biron

A long neglected and misunderstood area of American Indian art has been the identification, classification and dating of Northeast Woodland beadwork from the late eighteenth to the late nineteenth century. As an independent researcher of this beadwork for over two decades I have made some observations about beaded bags in particular that I believe shed some light on the material culture of the Northeast Woodland tribes. This essay will cover the broad variety of bags that were made throughout the nineteenth century, with a special focus on examples from the first half of that century. Early purses that incorporate linear designs, geometric shapes and organic motifs have become quite scarce and very collectible, but not everyone is aware of the historical context and currents that contributed to the emergence of this type of American Indian craftsmanship. The close relationship between these beaded bags and another cultural phenomenon – the rise of tourism at Niagara Falls – will here be examined.

1. Drawstring reticules, Haudenosaunee type, 1810s - 1830, from left to right; 7" high x 6" wide x 2.5" deep, 4.5" high x 3.4" square and 6.8" high x 3.3" square. Glass beads, broadcloth and silk ribbon. Three early drawstring reticules with heart, geometric, double-curve and four directional sun/star motifs. Because early nineteenth century Regency period ladies gowns did not provide room for pockets, women were compelled to carry necessary items in small drawstring bags called reticules. Precursor to the purse, the reticule provided a place to store important items such as spare change, a small mirror, handkerchief etc. Jeff Baird, photographer, Brattleboro, VT.

The first Europeans to set their sights on the New World were confronted with a people whose traditions and way of life were so different that, in retrospect, it was inevitable their cultures would clash. From the time of first contact and largely through the work of well meaning missionaries, a slow process of acculturation began to undermine the spiritual foundations of the Northeast Woodland people. Conflicts from King Philip's War to the American Revolution would facilitate the work of the missions, destroying not only the Indians' ancestral ties to the land, but their economic base as well, forever altering the lives and arts of these indigenous people.

The end of the Revolutionary War saw the beginning of two other revolutions that would also impact the lives and arts of the tribes from the Northeast. The first, tourism, was taking root as early as the eighteenth century. Americans and Europeans, intrigued by reports of picturesque spots such as Niagara Falls, the natural springs of Saratoga, and the coastal resort areas from Nova Scotia to New Jersey, were traveling to experience these sights directly. Meanwhile, a second revolution was taking place in the fashion world of Paris. By the end of the eighteenth century, women's apparel had become so bulky that it distended the female shape; that was about to change. During the reign of Napoleon (1804-1814), his first wife, Josephine, dramatically transformed European fashions. The preceding era's voluminous skirts evolved into a new thin and sheer style of women's dress. Pockets or pouches worn underneath the dress were now out of the question. A new bag had come into vogue, the stylish beaded reticule, or drawstring handbag. It could be worn outside the skirt, and it quickly became an essential article of women's attire. Figure 1 illustrates three early Iroquois reticules created for the sophisticated nineteenth-century traveler.

Indian women, wisely assessing the needs and ideas of the encroaching white population, found subsistence in increasingly difficult times by adapting their traditional skills, and by selling and trading their arts and crafts to suit the emerging Euro/American tourist market developing at Niagara Falls.

2. Beaded bags, Haudenosaunee type, 1810s - 1840s, approximately 7" high x 6" wide. Glass beads, broadcloth and silk ribbon. Group of seventeen Haudenosaunee bags in the classic hexagonal shape.

In so doing, they created a new art form: delicate, intricately beaded bags, hats, and other whimsical objects. The beadworkers came from diverse cultures and regions: the Haudenosaunee (Iroquois) of New York State and Canada and the Wabanaki of New England and the Maritime Provinces of Eastern Canada. Gifted with a refined sense of design, and sharing a passion for beadworking, they executed a profusion of bright, bold mosaics that included floral, figural, geometric, double curve, and sun/star symbol motifs. This "tourist" or "souvenir" art, as it's come to be called, played a crucial role in the subsistence of many Indian families during the nineteenth century. Above all, it was the convergence of these Indian beadworkers and tourists in the area of Niagara Falls that had a major influence on the production of beaded bags.

The Indian Settlements Around Niagara Falls

The last quarter of the eighteenth century witnessed the demise of the Iroquois Confederacy of upstate New York. In the years following General John Sullivan's 1779 "scorched earth" campaign against the Loyalists and their Iroquois supporters, some two thousand Iroquois refugees were settled along an eight-mile stretch of the road from the Falls to Lake Ontario.

By the end of the American Revolution, the power of the Iroquois Confederacy had been broken and they were no longer an effective organization. Many Iroquois, believing they would retain their traditional hunting grounds, had given their allegiance to the colonials' fight for independence. The new United States government did not keep that promise. Instead, reservations were established for the Seneca at Buffalo Creek (now Buffalo, NY) and at Tonawanda; the Tuscarora, who had been forced out of North Carolina earlier in the century, were granted land at Niagara Falls; the result for the Iroquois was a loss of access to vast areas of their traditional hunting grounds. Those who had supported the defeated British followed the Mohawk Chief, Joseph Brant, to Canada where they were granted a twelve-mile tract of land along the Grand River. This forced curtailment of their traditional life style and compelled them to find new ways to subsist. We may never know with certainty exactly when the Haudenosaunee began producing "souvenir art" but the dating of early tourist style bags suggest it began soon after they were removed to the reservations in Western New York.

Travelers to the area were confronted by the presence of the Haudnausaunee and, as we shall see, actually sought them out. The old tribal art customs that existed prior to the American Revolution changed and in many cases disappeared, to be replaced by the emergence of distinct local styles in each of the reservation communities. Souvenir bags from this early period display a level of craftsmanship and creativity that paralleled those in earlier artistic traditions. And it was the presence of Niagara Falls that attracted travelers who would indirectly influence the production of souvenir material by creating a market for it.

3. Stereograph, circa 1860s, 4.4" high x 7" wide. One panel from an imperial size stereograph by George Barker of Niagara Falls, NY. The descriptive caption reads: *Tuscarora Squaws - Luna Island - Niagara.* The lady standing on the far left is considering the purchase of a beaded purse. This stereograph is one in a series depicting Tuscarora women selling their beadwork to tourists at Niagara Falls.

Early Visitors to Niagara Falls

Ever since the first accounts of Niagara Falls, its majestic beauty and raw, wild power has captured the psyche of people from all parts of the world. The Recollet Friar Louis Hennepin first published a description of the cataract in 1678. Although an isolated spot, the French moved in quickly and continued to come there long after losing their domination of Canada to the British in the 1750s. Because of its strategic location, Niagara soon became a venue of commercial importance and a coveted gateway to the rich fur lands in the west. Engravings of the Falls sold briskly in the first half of the 18th century. Many of the early paintings of Niagara were done by artist-soldiers who had been stationed in Canada, and an engraving by R. Hancock, published in 1794, depicts stylish visitors enjoying the spectacle of the Falls (Seibel [1968] 1986:240). When the artist John Maude visited the site, in 1800, he was impressed by the bustling activity. He described a portage that employed numerous teams of oxen and that he passed great numbers of them on the road. Additionally, there were three schooners docked near Fort Niagara and fourteen teams of oxen waiting to be loaded (Severance 1903:79).

In addition to serving as a vital commercial junction, Niagara Falls also attracted some of the earliest European and American tourists. When a French nobleman visited Niagara in 1792, he described a cluster of one hundred houses and that there was a "tolerable inn" (Severance 1903:73). As early as 1795, guides were regularly taking travelers into the gorge below Niagara and early guide books describe cedar and pine trees that had been cut and lowered into the ravine by the Indians for use as ladders. The branches would be cut short and used as hand and footholds. Patrick Campbell, who traveled in the area in 1792 and 1793, reported that the shoreline of Lake Ontario from Niagara to Toronto was "all settled, and in some parts several concessions deep" (Campbell [1793] 1937:149).

Early travelers to the area, such as a Mrs. Simcoe who visited there in 1792 and again in 1795, were often entertained by the local gentry and as a treat were taken by sled or foot to see the Grand Falls of Niagara (Severance 1903:79-80). Mrs. Simcoe noted in her diary, dated May 24, 1795 that a "Mr.

4. Animal hide pouches, Haudenosaunee (?), first quarter of the nineteenth century. The smallest piece is 1.3" high x 1.6" wide and the largest is 6.3" high x 6.8" wide. Glass beads, silk ribbon and deer hide. The puzzle pouch on the far left has a silk ribbon edge trim and silk ribbon inlays. The large bag in the center has a silk lining, silk ribbon edge binding and once had a silk ribbon strap. The use of silk on the large bag suggests that it may have been intended for the tourist trade, making it an early transitional piece.

Pilkington was desired to place ladders to form a stairway down the bank" (as quoted in Seibel [1968] 1986:281). This ladder became known as Mrs. Simcoe's ladder and it remained in use by visitors until at least 1818.

Timothy Bigelow, an attorney from Massachusetts, set off from Boston in early July of 1805 to visit the celebrated Falls. Upon his arrival in late July he lodged at Gilbert's Hotel. He noted in his journal on July 27th that he and his traveling companions "were better fed than lodged at the hotel, on account of the number of guest we found there" (Bigelow, [1805] 1876:69). So even at this early date, Niagara was a place bustling with activity and visitors.

Attempts to Christianize the Indians at Niagara Falls

Meanwhile, foreign influences would also play a major role in the development of the beaded bags as a trade item: the Christian missionary movement. After Sullivan's expedition in 1779, as mentioned, many Iroquois were moved to permanent settlements in western New York. One of the earliest ventures to Christianize them came in the year 1800 when the New York Missionary Society sent the Rev.

Elkanah Holmes as a preacher to the Seneca and the Tuscaroras. His initial attempts met with little success as many Haudenosaunee, led by the Seneca chief and orator Red Jacket, were suspicious of the missions believing they were there to dispossess the Indian of what little land they had left. By 1820, the relentless work of the Christian missions had succeeded in the establishment of schools on the reservations and they were now instructing many Indians in both domestic and agricultural arts. The Rev. Thompson Harris, a missionary to the Indians at the Buffalo Creek Reservation, wrote in his journal on September 15, 1826, that several carriages a day were visiting the Indian mission schools. They were filled with travelers from Europe as well as America who were curious about the Indians and eager to learn about them (Severance 1903:151).

The work of missionaries had succeeded in dividing the western New York Iroquois into two major factions. Those who now subscribed to the teachings of the Bible were referred to as the Christian Party, while Red Jacket became the spokesman for a dissenting group of traditionalists who opposed the work of the missions. Both his group and the followers of Handsome Lake, the Seneca prophet and visionary, were referred to as the Pagan Party. Yet it is likely that each of these factions were producing beaded bags for sale to area visitors, and after a time each group had developed a distinctive style that was easily identifiable to their contemporaries. For instance, those purses with the highly stylized floral designs likely originated with, and in the end dominated the work of the Christian Party. Designs incorporating floral patterns were prevalent in European fashions and the mission school teachers were likely familiar with this. Certainly they would have suggested to their Iroquois students that souvenir items that incorporated the latest fashion trends would be more saleable to area visitors.

The adherents of the Pagan Party were more likely to maintain the status quo and, in so doing, to carry on with the traditional designs that we see on the hexagonal shaped bags. A broad selection of these with their linear designs and geometric shapes is illustrated in Figure 2. I believe this style of bag predates the floral ones by at least a quarter century and conceivably first appeared as early as the 1790's.

5. Beaded bag, Haudenosaunee type, circa 1807, approximately 6.5" high x 6" wide. Glass beads, broadcloth and silk ribbon. An Iroquois bag collected in Albany, NY in 1807 by Dennis Doyle, a merchant from New York City who was in Albany for the inaugural launch of Robert Fulton's steamboat, the *Claremont*. Acquired by the State Museum in Albany, NY in 1964 by a descendant of Doyle. NYSM catalog no. E-50500. George Hamell, photographer. Image copyright New York State Museum, Albany. Used with permission.

Tourism Takes Over at Niagara Falls

Americans were attracted to the Falls for different reasons. To many, the site represented a pure and pristine environment, which was seen as healthful and invigorating. To others it became a symbol, which fused, in a single image the nature, character and destiny of America. Many who came to Niagara also saw the Indian as a symbol of this untamed wilderness. But none of this could stop the developing commercialization of the Falls as a sensational curiosity for tourists.

In 1818, William Forsyth erected an elevated structure with stairs and a covered roof to allow visitors a better view of the spectacle (Siebel [1968] 1986:261). If he charged for the occasion then this may have been the first commercial tourist venture at Niagara. After the completion of the Erie Canal, in 1825, the area became much more accessible and two years later, an entrepreneur staged an event, which attracted thousands of people. A boat filled with a variety of animals was sent over the cataract to see if any would swim to safety. Unfortunately, only a duck and a pig survived but stunts like this attracted numerous visitors to the Falls and a circus atmosphere soon became the prevailing character there.

In 1827, a Mr. Barnett opened a museum to take advantage of the increasing number of tourists visiting the area. Along with the stuffed animals, insects, and minerals on display was a selection of Indian curiosities. In a guidebook published in 1839, the Tuscarora Reservation is listed as one of the area attractions. One tourist observed that after taking a look into their wigwams, that they "make such observations, and take such notes of the customs and manners of the inhabitants, as a short and hasty visit affords; purchase some articles of Indian manufacture; or perhaps, seek an introduction to the venerable chief" (DeVeaux 1839:110).

6. Beaded bag, Haudenosaunee type, first quarter of the nineteenth century, 6.8" high x 6.4" wide. Glass beads, broadcloth and silk ribbon. A classic hexagonal bag with the central star/sun and four-directional cross. The verso has a central diamond and double curve motifs.

By 1833, visitors were overwhelmed by the rapid expansion of tourist attractions and were noting their objections to the proposed development of the Canadian side. Railroad connections to the Falls were completed in the 1830s and with the construction of a bridge to the Canadian side in 1848, the area was now described as overrun by rank, bad taste, and old curiosity shops. Yet simultaneous with this there was emerging a more respectable trade in Indian wares that would contribute to the preservation of the beaded bags now so prized by collectors.

A Fascination for Anything Indian

Early records indicate that Europeans have had an affinity with Indian attire since first contact. Traders quickly recognized the superiority of Indian clothing and it was soon adopted for their own use. Voyagers, trappers and peddlers of every sort wore moccasins decorated with beads or quills, as well as leggings and decorated hide jackets. Soldiers were also fascinated with Indian attire, as several 18th century paintings will attest, and although the widespread use of such apparel was against regulations, many of them wore moccasins and often acquired quilled and beaded Indian items as souvenirs.

It is well known that late-eighteenth and early-nineteenth century travelers to remote and exotic destinations were enthusiastic about collecting natural history specimens. Two of the guests whom Bigelow encountered at Gilbert's Hotel were a doctor from Philadelphia and a gentleman from Baltimore, both of whom were mineralogists collecting fossils and mineral specimens on their trip. This collecting spirit often included the acquisition of ethnographic items as well.

Jasper Grant traveled throughout the Great Lakes area in the late seventeenth and early eighteenth centuries and amassed a large collection of Woodland Indian art, some of which was from the Niagara Falls area (Phillips 1984:19). Isaac Weld, who traveled to Quebec between 1795-1797, visited the convent of the Ursiline nuns where Indian girls were being schooled. He wrote how the nuns were embroidering curious looking articles made in the Indian fashion. He referred to such items as pocket-books, work baskets, etc. and what he described as some "very curious bark-work" which he said they embroidered with elk hair and dyed of the most brilliant colors. Weld said they also made models of Indian canoes and other related items that were available for sale to visitors and how it was always expected of travelers to purchase some little souvenir to help them out (Weld 1807:16-17).

By 1841, the sale of Indian objects at the Falls was in full swing. To take advantage of this, the Hulett brothers opened the first of two Indian curiosity shops. In their 1844 guidebook they indicate that they

> …have made arrangements with the traders of most of the Indian tribes in North America, for a constant supply of their choicest manufactures; among some of the articles will be found – bead work of every description, bark work beautifully embroidered with moose hair and porcupine quills, such as card cases, card receivers, boxes, cigar cases, bark shoes and gloves, canoes, wampum belts, ladies belts, etc. etc. from the Esquimaux, Labrador and North Western tribes of Indians, direct from the Indian traders; also beautiful moccasin work from the Conewaga, St. Regis and Lake of the Two Mountain Indians. Examine these selections before purchasing elsewhere; some visitors have purchased Indian work at Buffalo, not knowing that Niagara Falls is the greatest market for splendid Indian work of every variety, in the United States. The Seneca, Tonawanda, Tuscarora, Allegany and Cattaraugus Indians invariably bring their manufactures to Niagara Falls for sale; the refuse that will not sell to the dealers at the Falls, is taken to Buffalo, and there traded off for goods, being of a very inferior quality (Hulett 1844:46).

There were other purveyors of Indian art at Niagara Falls. Fox's Curiosity Shop opened around 1843 and two decades later it was still doing a brisk business. A local newspaper wrote that

> Those who pass over the bridge spanning the rapids – and what visitor to the Falls will omit to do this! – should pass at the Indian store of Mr. Fox, at the toll-gate, and examine the endless variety of exquisitely wrought Indian work which he offers for inspection and sale. He has some articles which are entirely new – perfect miracles in the ingenuity of their design and beauty of workmanship *(Niagara Falls Gazette.* July 15, 1863*)*.

By 1855, when the world's first suspension bridge was completed across the gorge, there were approximately 60,000 travelers a year visiting Niagara (Donaldson 1979:152). By this time, the sale of beadwork and other Indian souvenirs was taking place on both sides of the Falls. A ladies handbook from the period wrote that "The beadwork of the North American Indians is among the most beautiful. The Canadian Indian women sell large quantities to visitors to the Falls of Niagara, and a great deal of it finds its way to our large cities" (Hartley 1859:25). In Figure 3, a stylish Victorian lady considers the purchase of a small beaded purse from a Tuscarora woman at Niagara Falls in the 1860s.

7. Beaded bag, Haudenosaunee type, circa 1822, 6.9" high x 6.3" wide. Glass beads, broadcloth and silk ribbon.

The days when the Indians made the long and dangerous trading journey by canoe, to distant outposts, was gone. The nineteenth century saw a new breed of Indian trader, one who traveled to remote destinations, not by foot or canoe but rather by the most modern of inventions. An upstate New York newspaper account from 1859 recorded such a journey:[1]

> "Lo! The Poor Indian." Pope would not have made such a remark had he been in this city yesterday, and looked upon a party of a dozen or more Indians of the St. Regis tribe, who arrived on the steamer Ontario from one of

8. Beaded bags, Haudenosaunee type, 1825 - 1840s, approximately 7" high x 6" wide. Glass beads, broadcloth and silk ribbon.

9. Beaded bags, calling card wallets and a Glengarry hat, Haudenosaunee type, late 1840s to 1870s. The bags are approximately 6.5" high x 5.5" wide, calling card wallets are approximately 7" long x 4.5" wide and the hat is 11" long x 6.1" wide. Glass beads, velvet and cotton fabric. Classic group of floral pieces with figural elements. Some contemporary Tuscarora beadworkers refer to these beaded birds as Carolina parakeets, the extinct birds that once lived in their North Carolina homeland before the Tuscarora moved north.

the St. Lawrence ports. These people were generally between twenty and thirty years of age – the sexes nearly equal – and were as tidy and comely Indians as we ever saw. They were dressed after the fashion of the Lower Canadian Indians, but their clothing was well made and quite becoming – if a squaw with pantaloons, moccasins and a tight-fitting cloak, with a sort of cowl for the head, can appear becoming. This party had with them nearly a ton of baggage in trunks, and took tickets to the west from Mr. Darlings Union Ticket office. On inquiry, we ascertained that these Indians are on a trading mission for their tribe to the southwest. They will stop at St. Louis while others will go to New Orleans and intermediate places. In those cities they will remain during the coming winter selling the trinkets and curious articles of Indian manufacture which they have with them, and which may be sent on by the tribe. These visits to the South for trading purposes are annually made by representatives of this tribe. This fact may surprise many, as it may be supposed that the Mississippi markets would be overrun with Indian products from the tribes who live upon its great tributaries. But the old St. Regis tribe of Christian Indians of New York can find a market for their goods on the Mississippi, and those who purchase them may fancy that they were made in the wigwams of the far west by quite a different class of natives. The St. Regis tribe resides in the village by that name in Franklin county, near the Canada line (from the *Rochester Union and Advertiser*, November 12, 1859).

10. Daguerreotype, circa 1850, 3.2" high x 2.8" wide. Engaging portrait of a young woman with an early Iroquois floral bag.

A Description of Early Souvenir Bags

The modern era of glass bead manufacture began in Europe at the end of the twelfth century and quickly became an important trade item for Europeans. Glass beads were among the first European commodities brought to the New World and they would eventually replace the quill, shell and other natural materials that the Indians used for decorating clothing and other personal items.

To the Northeast Woodland People, the technical advantages and potential for creative expression made beads increasingly desirable. Although initial supplies were limited, there is evidence from the earliest contacts with traders that the Indians were indicating a preference for white, blue and purple beads. These were the colors they were accustomed to working with in wampum (shell) and no doubt it influenced their preference for trade beads. As early as 1726, the James Bay Cree of Canada were placing yearly orders for two hundred pounds of beads from Fort Albany and were specifying that they be white and purple and "the smaller the better" (Oberholtzer, 1991:20).

Among the Northeast Woodland tribes, there were three major groups using this new medium to create their artwork:

- The Haudenosaunee (Iroquois) of Western New York such as the Seneca and Tuscarora and those Iroquois living on the nearby Six Nations Reserve in Brantford, Ontario.
- The Wabanaki from eastern Canada and the

maritime area, which included the Penobscot, Passamaquoddy, Maliseet and Mi'kmaq.

- A mixed group of Indians (primarily Mohawks) and western Abenakis from the Indian reserves near Montreal such as at Akwesasne (St Regis) and Kahnawake (Caughnawaga).

We are inclined to use terms like Mohawk, Seneca, Tuscarora, Mi'kmaq, Maliseet, etc. in our desire to specifically attribute an object. Because of the overlapping styles among these groups, assigning a piece to a regional form such as Haudenosaunee type, or Kahnawake type, or Wabanaki type would be less problematic.

Regardless of our method of attributing this work, before the opening of the Erie Canal, the likelihood is that the Seneca and Tuscarora were the only people selling beadwork at Niagara Falls and some of the first beaded items they sold to tourists were likely bags. The earliest known bags or pouches created by the Iroquois were made of hide and they were decorated with porcupine quills. Figure 4 illustrates several early hide bags that were decorated with seed beads. The three smaller ones are generally referred to as puzzle pouches. Both the Algonquian and Iroquoian peoples of the Northeast woodlands produced this style of coin purse. These examples date from the first quarter of the 19th century. The body of the bag on the lower left is decorated with porcelain white, translucent blue and crystal beads and is edged with a green silk ribbon and silk ribbon inlays. Like many early examples of Northeastern beaded bags, the overall field is generally monochromatic with the internal designs created in all white or white and blue beadwork in a strictly linear fashion (see inside front and back covers).

11. Beaded bag, Haudenosaunee type, circa 1830s, 7" high x 6.75" wide. Glass beads, broadcloth and silk ribbon. The design of this bag incorporates a rudimentary form of the common floral motifs that would later predominate the beadwork of the Iroquois in the second half of the nineteenth century.

The bag on the lower right is similarly decorated with white and blue beads and a scattering of other colors. It was acquired from a Massachusetts estate and had an old, faded, hand written note inside that reads: "My grandfather bought this [bag] when he was peddling wooden ware out west [Niagara Falls?] among the Indians of an Indian girl." The double puzzle pouch in the lower center is unlike any other in my experience and its diminutive size suggests that it may have been made for a doll.

The large hide bag in Figure 4 is totally decorated with white beads. The edge of the bag has a reddish/pink (now much faded) silk ribbon binding with similar silk ribbon inlays on both the front and back faces of the bag. Lined with an olive green silk fabric, it originally had a silk ribbon carrying strap. Ted Brasser attributes it to the Seneca and ascribes a circa 1800 origin to this piece.[2] I believe it could be the archetype for the beaded bags on fabric that would soon be made for the emerging tourist markets in the Northeast. The six-pointed star is intriguing as each arm has a silk ribbon inlay that is outlined in tiny white beads. This same bag is stylistically similar to a "Seneca" piece illustrated in Lyford 1945:72, Figure 63. It's likely the Iroquois were doing this type of silk inlay during the same period that the Mi'kmaq were developing their very fine silk appliqué, and the Midwestern tribes their very bold ribbonwork. I know of no other examples of this type of bag.

Dating this early material can be unsettling at times given the nature of the available evidence. But from those few examples that do exist, I believe a reasonable assessment can be made.

Perhaps the best documented bag I am familiar with is the one in Figure 5, in the collection of the New York State Museum in Albany, New York. Acquired by the museum in 1964, it was originally

12. Beaded bags, Wabanaki type, 1850s - 1870s, approximately 6" high x 5.5" wide. Glass beads, broadcloth, velvet and silk ribbon. The circular object between the lower two bags is a pen wipe.

purchased in 1807 from an Indian in Albany, New York, by Dennis Doyle, a New York City merchant. He went there as a guest of Robert Fulton for the maiden voyage of Fulton's steamboat, the *Clermont.* Dennis Doyle was the uncle of Mrs. Charles M. Purdy, of Marlborough, Massachusetts, whose name was inscribed on an old note inside the bag where she identified it as once belonging to Doyle. Mrs. Purdy's granddaughter subsequently acquired the bag from her grandmother and upon the granddaughter's death a friend donated it to the museum. This bag has what I consider to be the classic Haudenosaunee hexagonal shape. Its linear simplicity incorporates alternating strings of beads in the outer bands and a large central heart, a motif often seen on early Haudenosaunee bags. The designs are all linear, with no areas of solid bead fill.

13. Beaded bags, Wabanaki type, 1830s - 1850s, approximately 6.5" high x 5.5" wide. Glass beads, velvet, silk ribbon and bilaterally symmetrical designs.

The flaps have three representations of a sun/star motif encircling an equal-armed cross. Scholars have interpreted the use of this design among the woodland tribes as symbolizing the four cardinal directions. To communicate with the spirits, one had to first locate the central axis of the universe, generally considered to be at the center of the four directions. As such, this symbol, often seen on early bags, may represent a gateway into the spirit world.

Thirty years after Doyle purchased his bag in Albany an interesting advertisement appeared in a newspaper from the same city announcing the sale of Indian beaded bags at S. Van Schaack's variety store on South Market Street (*The Daily Albany Argus*, January 17, 1837). This is the earliest printed advertisement that I'm aware of that offered what were likely Iroquois beaded bags for sale.

The bag in Figure 6 had the following note inside it, in old faded script. "This bag was given to me in August, 1919 by Miss Blake of Cape May [New Jersey] – She is 88 years old and said the bag was brought from Niagara Falls 125 years ago by a relative. It was made by Indian women – Grace May Lissenden." If Miss Blake's recollection was accurate, it would date this piece to 1794. Certainly it is from the same period as the Dennis Doyle bag as stylistically it is quite similar, having the hexagonal body shape, the sun/star motif with equal-armed cross and the alternating strings of beads in both a linear and zigzag pattern. Additionally it has the double curve motif and a central diamond or square on the reverse, which some scholars identify as a symbol representing the central fire of the Haudenosaunee. It has the linear simplicity of the Doyle bag and does not incorporate any areas of solid bead fill.

Figure 7 illustrates a type of bag that I refer to as a False Face bag because the design elements are arranged in a way that is reminiscent of the contorted faces we find on Iroquois False Face masks. I don't pretend to know if there was a relationship between the designs of this bag and the False Face Society but I have seen numerous examples of this type and so only use the term descriptively.

This particular example, stylistically similar to the two bags just described, has the familiar motifs of these early period purses worked into the shape of a distorted face. A separation between the bag face and the inside lining revealed a fragment of an old newspaper, no doubt used to stiffen the bag during construction, and it was dated May 14, 1822.

The beadwork produced by the three major groups is distinctive and changed stylistically over time. Those changes occurred gradually but as a general rule, noticeable style refinements can be categorized and placed into quarter century timeframes.

A characteristic of virtually all early (pre-1850) Iroquois bags is that a different design is used on each face. Cataloged examples in many museums as well as in published sources indicate that it was either the Seneca or Tuscarora of western New York that were making the majority of the hexagonally shaped bags. The traveling exhibit "Across Borders: Beadwork in Iroquois Life" (2001-2003) featured several hexagonal shaped bags identified as Iroquois, one of which had the date 1830 stitched in beads across the front. A study of the oldest dated pieces suggest that the earliest bags in the study (1800 – 1825) were often hexagonal in shape, had relatively simple, linear designs, and often incorporated the double-curve, heart, diamond and the four-directional sun/star motifs. The earliest bags also appear to have had no solid areas of bead fill. The fabric ground that bags were beaded on was almost exclusively red or black broadcloth and the ribbon trim was almost always made of silk, most often green or red. Additionally, most of the hexagonally shaped bags I have studied also had a beaded stitch sewn along the outside edge of the silk ribbon binding. Very early souvenir bags don't have the technical refinement that later bags have, perhaps because the use of beadwork on broadcloth at this time was a relatively new skill.

The completion of the Erie Canal in 1825 not only brought more sightseers to Niagara but this event may have opened the way for competition from other tribal people as well. This caused numerous scenarios to develop, resulting in the beaders' work becoming more intricate and technical as they competed with one another for the tourist trade. After 1825, designs still incorporated the geometric and organic motifs of the earlier period but the use of finer beads allowed for more elaborate designs to be executed. After this date we gradually see the use of solidly filled design areas as well. There are a number of reasons why this may have happened. One artist may have deliberately created pieces that were more intricate than another's work in order to make her creations more attractive and desirable to a potential patron. Or, as time progressed, the artists became more skillful in their craft, the natural outcome of which was a more elaborate and beautifully executed piece. I place these bags in the second period of the study (1825-1850). In most cases, bags from this period, such as those in Figure 8, have a lot of similarities with earlier period pieces but as a general rule, they are more refined, often use smaller beads and have areas of solid bead fill. These quarter century time frames are not hard and fast rules but are rather intended as a general guide in dating this material.

14. Beaded bags, Kahnawake Mohawk(?), 1840s to 1915. Sizes range from 7.9" wide x 7.9" high to 5.5" high x 6.75" wide. Glass beads, cotton and velvet fabric. A group of bags that incorporate a large and perhaps characteristic floral motif.

By the late 1840s, a design transformation was taking place in Iroquois beadwork. The geometric and organic motifs on pre-1850 material gave way to a preponderance of floral designs. Deborah Harding, in her Master's thesis on Iroquois beaded bags (Harding, April 1994),[3] proposed that the floral motifs may have been inspired by those on Berlin Work, a form of embroidery that was the craze in the mid-nineteenth century. The bags from the early floral period (late 1840s to late 1850s), see Figure 9, generally had long stems, smaller flowers, and finer beads than later examples (late 1850s – 1890s) and the earliest designs were often bilaterally symmetrical. Some contemporary Tuscarora beadworkers refer to the beaded birds seen on the examples in Figure 9 as Carolina parakeets, alluding to the extinct birds that once lived in their North Carolina homeland before the Tuscarora moved north.

An early floral bag with long stems and small flowers and dated 1849 is illustrated in *Trading Identities – The Souvenir in Native North American Art from the Northeast, 1700 – 1900*, by Ruth Phillips, Plate 6. Take note of the long stems on the floral bag in Figure 10, a circa 1850 daguerreotype. Even at this early date, the floral patterns on this bag are well developed into the recognizable style of bags that were produced by the Iroquois in the second half of the nineteenth century. Examples in other daguerreotype and ambrotype images substantiate this early date for floral bags and they indicate that this decorative style of beading was routinely being made in the 1850s.

An earlier, circa 1830s bag made in the classic Haudenosaunee hexagonal shape may be the genesis of this floral tradition. In the central panel of the bag in Figure 11 is a rudimentary form of this floral style. It's intriguing to think that the post-1850 bags could have been inspired by the artist who created this particular piece.

Later bags and hats dating from the late 1850s to the 1890s have increasingly shorter stems or no stems at all and with the passage of time use progressively larger beads. The floral designs from this later period tend to be asymmetrical as well. The use of rickrack trim and tubular beads is also seen on pieces from this period. Unlike the linear and geometric bags from the pre-1850 period, virtually all of the post-1850 Iroquois floral bags also have the same design on both faces of the bag and the vast majority of them use a red cotton ribbon edge binding. Post-1850 bags in this decorative tradition often incorporate brass

15. Beaded bag, Mohawk(?), circa 1840s, 6.3" high (not including the strap) x 5.8" wide. An early beaded bag possibly from one of the Mohawk Reserves near Montreal. The two beehive-like motifs in the upper corners have been attributed to the Mohawk in other examples I have seen. The two figures wearing top hats look similar to those in a lithograph from the Public Archives of Canada, Ottawa that was published in 1841 by Henry D. Thielcke titled *The Presentation of a Newly Elected Chief of the Huron Tribe, Canada.* The beaver pelt top hat was part of the formal dress of many Northeast Woodland people during the mid-nineteenth century.

sequins in their designs, a feature that is noticeably absent on pre-1850 material.

Wabanaki bags from the Maritime area, like those pictured in Figure 12, have common features as well. As a general rule, their contour is in the form of an upside-down keyhole shape though there are exceptions to this. Examples in the Canadian Museum of Civilization, the Maine State Museum and other institutions are attributed to the Maliseet although pieces with similar motifs have also been noted on known Mi'kmaq material.

The flowers and leaf patterns on Wabanaki bags are stylistically distinctive. The flowers can have as few as five and as many as fifteen petals and these often have squared off ends. The leaf patterns are also unique as they are usually ovate or in the shape of a heart and almost always fully beaded. The main stem is generally made up from a flat bundle of beaded strings, usually in white, each of which connects to either a flower or leaf in the design. This stem originates from a central point at the base of the bag and often has bi-lobed or tri-lobed buds or ears connected to it. Occasionally, bags from this area have a beaded fringe hanging from the lower edge binding and sometimes there is a section of twisted fringe along a top panel. As a general rule, Wabanaki bags don't incorporate the use of a beaded chain stitch along the outside edge binding of the bag, as is more often the case in Iroquois examples. Pre-1850 bags from this area are rare. The examples in Figure 13 have relatively linear designs, unlike the later examples that almost exclusively incorporate the use of solid bead fill in their execution. The earliest Wabanaki bags are usually bilaterally symmetrical whereas the designs on those from the latter half of the century tend to be asymmetrical.

Because a particular purse is identified as Maliseet or Mi'kmaq doesn't mean that every comparable example can be similarly attributed. Consider a pouch made by an elderly Nehantic woman from Connecticut called Mercy Nonsuch. In 1912, she was photographed holding a keyhole shaped bag that the anthropologist Frank Speck described as an example of her handiwork (see: Speck 1928, plate 18). This style of bag is generally attributed to the Wabanaki, not the Nehantic. Was this an original design or simply a copy of one she saw and admired? It certainly is the anomaly.

It is impossible to know how common it was for one Indian artist to copy the work of another, as there is not enough evidence available to support a conclusion. This practice, if it was widespread, only adds to the misunderstanding about this material.

The earliest beaded bags produced by the Indian groups in the Montreal area appears to originate from the 1830s or 1840s and by the turn of the century their beadwork becomes quite bold and distinctive. Later pieces, like the example in the top of Figure 14 (both front and back shown), incorporate strong colors and large beads in a baroque style. The fabric ground upon which the beads were sewn is often a hot pink, purple or tan or some other striking color.

Earlier mid-century pieces like the lower examples in Figure 14 are also distinctive but attribution was derived deductively. The cuffs on a pair of moccasins in the collection of the anthropologist Frank Bergevin are done in the same beading style and incorporate floral motifs like the ones on these bags, but they were missing the vamps. The paper stiffeners were still on the moccasins and they were from a Montreal area newspaper. Bergevin said he showed these to a noted Mi'kmaq scholar in Nova Scotia and she said they definitely were not Mi'kmaq. So he took them to an Abenaki Reserve and his informants there said they definitely weren't Western Abenaki.

Additionally, I have seen specific designs on other bags, like the beehive motifs in the upper corners of Figure 15, that were attributed to the Mohawk and those pieces had other design elements on them that are very similar to some found on the bags in Figure 14. So these may very well be from Kahnawake or from one of the other Mohawk Reserves in the Montreal area. The large floral motifs on these bags are also similar to those observed on several nineteenth century cabinet cards of Kahnawake Mohawks dressed in their finest attire. I've yet to see an early documented Kahnawake bag so this is an area still in need of study.

Conclusion

There are other distinctive styles of Northeast Woodland bags that have not been discussed here. Certainly there were many Indians engaged in the production of beadwork during the nineteenth century and not all of them had the same degree of skill or conformed to the stylized design formulas I have presented here. Many of the distinctive and singularly styled pieces we see today could have been the product of an imaginative experiment or simply a design concept that never really took off. One thing is for certain: this was an art of survival. This early material has a spiritual quality about it that is akin to fine art. Inaugurated at a time when the

Northeastern tribes were impoverished and struggling to continue under conditions of devastating cultural loss, each piece was the product of hard work. Endowed with sacred values, the design motifs on the bags are steeped in the mystical worldview of the Northeast Woodland people. The Mi'kmaq in particular believed that there was power and magic in the decorations they placed on their attire. An artistic representation of a sacred plant, for instance, had a protective effect upon the wearer that was as powerful as the plant itself. Consequently, many Mi'kmaq garments and personal adornments had these designs woven into them.

As they worked in a communal setting, the beaders thoughtfully wove stories into their designs, which told of what it meant to be Haudenosaunee or Wabanaki. On the surface, these pieces were the canvas upon which an Indian artist displayed her technical skills and artistic vision. But below the surface, the power inherent in a beautiful object was a central feature of life. Festive dress was a language through which many an artist expressed her deepest beliefs about the universe. We may never know the full extent of their meanings, but imbedded within the designs are stories of a people told in symbols and motifs that spoke of a sacred relationship to the natural world. Many such stories are lost now, but the art survives as a legacy testifying to the inventiveness and sense of beauty of a forgotten people.

Endnotes

[1] My gratitude to George Hamell at the State Museum in Albany, NY for his scholarship in uncovering this article and for bringing it to my attention.

[2] Personal correspondence on November 7, 1996.

[3] I extend my thanks to Deborah Harding for sending me a copy of her thesis.

Bibliography

Bigelow, Timothy
1876 *Journal of a Tour to Niagara Falls in the Year 1805, with an Introduction by a Grandson.* Press of John Wilson and Sons, Boston.

Campbell, Patrick
1793 *Travels in North America in the Years 1791 and 1792.* The Champlain Society Toronto.

DeVeaux, S.
1839 *The Falls of Niagara or Tourist Guide to the Wonder of Nature,* William B. Hayden, Buffalo.

Donaldson, Gordon
1979 *Niagara! The Eternal Circus.* Doubleday, New York.

Harding, Deborah
1994 *Bagging the Tourist Market: A Descriptive and Statistical Study of 19th Century Iroquois Beaded Bags.* Unpublished Masters Thesis. np, np.

Hartley, Florence
1859 *Ladies Handbook of Fancy and Ornamental Work.* John E. Potter, Philadelphia.

Hulett, Theodore
1844 *Every Man His Own Guide to the Falls of Niagara or the Whole Story in a Few Words.* Faxon, Buffalo.

Lyford, Carrie
1945 *Iroquois Crafts.* The United States Department of the Interior. Bureau of Indian Affairs, Washington, DC.

Oberholtzer, Cath
1991 Embedded in Symbolism, The James Bay Beaded Hoods. *Northeast Indian Quarterly,* Vol. VIII, No. 2. The American Indian Program, Cornell University, Ithaca NY.

Phillips, Ruth
1984 *Patterns of Power, The Jasper Grant Collection and Great Lakes Indian Art of the Early 19th Century.* Catalog to the McMichael Canadian Collection, (October 14, 1984 through March 17, 1985), Kleinburg.
1998 *Trading Identities: The Souvenir in Native North American Art from the Northeast, 1700-1900.* University of Washington Press, Seattle and London: McGill-Queen's University Press, Montreal and Kingston.

Seibel, George
1968 *Niagara, River of Fame.* The Kiwanis Club of Stamford, Inc., Niagara Falls, Ontario, Canada.

Severance, Frank
1903 *Publications of the Buffalo Historical Society,* Vol. VI. The Buffalo Historical Society, Buffalo NY.

Speck, Frank
1928 Native Tribes and Dialects of Connecticut – a Mohegan-Pequot Diary. *Forty-Third Annual Report of the Bureau of American Ethnology, 1925-26.* US Government Printing Office, Washington, DC.

Weld, Isaac
1807 *Travels Through the States of North America and the Provinces of Upper and Lower Canada During the Years 1795, 1796, and 1797.* Fourth Edition, Vol. II. Printed for John Stockdale, Piccadilly, London.

Gallery

My career as a fine artist spans almost five decades and during that time I've exhibited my artwork in hundreds of shows nationwide, where my portraits of native people have won numerous "First Place" and "Best of Show" awards. My interest in the Indians of the Northeast stems primarily from my ancestry – my matrilineal great-grandmother Clarissa Basque was a Mi'kmaq from Nova Scotia. Though she died before I was born, her influence on my life has been profound as it's shaped and directed the nature of my work.

It was during the early 1980s while doing the research for a portrait of King Philip, the celebrated seventeenth-century chief of the Wampanoags from eastern Massachusetts that I discovered the splendid beadwork that was produced by the Northeast Woodland tribes. Gifted with a refined sense of color and design, and passionate about beadwork, these unacknowledged artists created a profusion of bright, bold mosaics that included floral, figurative, and geometric motifs. By adapting their traditional skills, they produced a form of survival art that was sold in tourist and collector markets from Niagara Falls to Nova Scotia and all the way south to New Orleans.

15a. Portrait of Clarissa Basque, great-grandmother of the author. My portrait honors her spirit as well as that of all the Northeast Woodland people whose history and images I portray in my work.

The discovery of an old photograph of a Seneca woman wearing a similar bag to those I collected led to further inquiry and I subsequently uncovered additional images of Indian people making and selling their beadwork. I was at last able to put faces on the artists whose work I admired. As I found more and more images it became apparent that I should tell their story by highlighting their beadwork in my paintings.

I'm grateful to both the Abbe Museum and the Memorial Hall Museum for allowing me to share my vision of this work. This exhibit and catalog is my tribute to the artists who produced this exquisite material.

Gerry Biron

16. Beaded bags and a pincushion, Haudenosaunee type, 1810s - 1830s, the bag at the top is 7" high x 6.9" wide. These examples incorporate the heart motif, a design element that is often seen on early Haudenosaunee bags. A variation of this heart motif is referred to as the national badge of the Iroquois by one Iroquois scholar (Lyford, 1945:69).

17. Figurative beaded bags. Clockwise from the top:
    - Haudenosaunee (?), circa 1830s, 8.5" high x 6.4" wide, tanned deer hide with an extended silk top, thunderbird motif on the front and a large, central floral design on the verso.
    - Haudenosaunee type, late 1820s - 1830s, 6.9" high x 6.2" wide, on broadcloth. A hexagonal bag with two female (?) figures holding hands; the negative space between them is in the shape of a heart. The verso has a large, eight petal flower motif (see the upper left bag in Figure 21).
    - Haudenosaunee type, circa 1830, 6.25" wide x 5.8" high, on black velvet. The lodge building motif is unique in my experience.
    - Northeast Woodlands type, second half of the nineteenth century, 4.8" wide x 6.6" high, red broadcloth. This rare form, in the shape of a house, has a silk lining decorated with an embroidered bird.
    - Center bag, Haudenosaunee type, circa 1830s, 6.7" wide and 6.2" high, black velvet with silk ribbon edge binding. The crown and shield motif suggests a Canadian origin and this piece may be from the Six Nations Reserve near Brantford, Ontario. The verso is the center bag in Figure 16.

18. Beaded bag, Haudenosaunee type, circa 1830, 6.2" wide x 6.5" high, broadcloth and silk ribbon. The figures on this piece may depict the good and evil twins from the Iroquois creation story. The design on the verso is suggestive of a face and the connected diamond motifs have silk inlays.

19. Beaded bag, possibly Mohawk from one of the Iroquois Reserves near Montreal, circa 1840s, 6.3" high (not including the strap) x 5.8" wide, black velvet. The two figures wearing top hats look similar to those in a lithograph from the Public Archives of Canada, Ottawa that was published in 1841 by Henry D. Thielcke titled *The Presentation of a Newly Elected Chief of the Huron Tribe, Canada*. The beaver pelt top hat was part of the formal dress of many Northeast Woodland people during the mid 19th century. The large fabric loop at the top of the bag allowed it to hang from a waist belt.

20. Beaded bag, Haudenosaunee type, circa 1840s, 6.8" wide x 6.5" high. This bag, with the scalloped lower edge, is one of only two examples I have encountered that is figurative on both sides. The figure on the left is leading a dog on a leash; the one on the right appears to be holding a basket. In my experience, the depiction of four birds perched in a tree is unique in Haudenosaunee art.

21. Beaded bags, Haudenosaunee type, 1820s to 1840s. The bag in the top row on the left is circa 1830, 7.9" wide x 7.3" high, silk inlays inside the four central diamond motifs. The center bag (both sides shown), 6.6" wide x 5.6" high is similar in style to one on a famous Daguerreotype of Caroline Parker, a noted Seneca beadworker who lived on the Tonawanda Reserve near Niagara Falls during the 1840s. The bottom bag with the extended top (both sides shown), 1830s-1840s, 6.3" wide x 9.3" high is uncommon as it is beaded on black silk and has a black silk ribbon edge trim. It's also unusual in that is has a floral motif on one side and a large, central sun design on the other.

22. Beaded bags, Iroquois type, averaging 6" wide x 5.75" high (except for the center bag), decorated in beads and moosehair, may be from a group of Seneca who were removed to Sandusky (Ohio) in the early nineteenth century. This attribution is based on a very similar bag and a pair of moccasins in the Rochester (NY) Museum and Science Center that was attributed to the Seneca of Sandusky by the donor. This group of Seneca was later removed to Oklahoma in the winter of 1831-32. The Iroquois Museum in Howes Caves, New York attributes a similarly styled bag in their collection (#37161) to the Tuscarora. Arthur C. Parker, the noted Seneca archaeologist and ethnographer, illustrates a similar bag in the American Anthropologist, Vol. 14, 1912, Plate XXXV that he identifies as Iroquois. Douglas Ewing dates another similar example, decorated in moosehair, like the examples on the top left and right of this figure, to the 1820s. See: The Spirit Sings, Plate 256. The moosehair on the upper left bag is sewn onto a deep blue silk.

The large bag in the center, 11.3" high x 14.7" wide, is unique and difficult to date but possibly from the mid-nineteenth century. It was from the estate of William Waldegrave Palmer – 2nd Earl of Selborne and high commissioner to Africa, and likely a presentation piece. A common characteristic of all these bags is the wide bands of beads that run along the scalloped perimeter. It's possible that this floral style originated in the Christian Party discussed in the essay.

23. Beaded bags. The top center bag, 1830s-1840s, 6.6" wide x 8.2" high, has a central design element that looks Delaware yet the beaded zigzag strings that surround it look Iroquois. It might be a hybrid form from the Six Nations Reserve near Brantford, Ontario where there were Delaware living among the Iroquois in the first half of the nineteenth century. The beaded bag in the middle row on the right, 1800-1830, 6.25" wide x 5.1" high, is unusual in that both sides were beaded on a single piece of broadcloth that was then folded over to create the bag. The bottom edge has no seam and the beaded design on the face of the bag flows continuously from one side to the other. The bottom bag is likely Haudenosaunee, circa 1840s, 5.5" wide x 6.2" high. The extended top and edge seam binding is done in black silk. The front of this bag is very unusual in that it has the name "Jane" stitched onto the bag in beads. I've never encountered another with a name on it. The anthropomorphic design on the verso is intriguing as well.

24. Man's cap, Canadian Wabanaki type, possibly Mi'kmaq, circa 1860s, 8" wide x 8.5" long x 5.5" high. A similar example was made by Mary Ann Geneace of Richibucto, New Brunswick in the second half of the nineteenth century. This example has much finer beads than the Geneace example and I believe it is a little earlier. See: The Spirit Sings – Artistic Traditions of Canada's First Peoples, McCelland and Steward, Glenbow Museum, 1987, page 47.

25. Canadian Wabanaki cap, possibly Maliseet, third quarter of the nineteenth century, 7.5" wide x 4.5" high. This piece is similar to two six-panel hats in the Canadian Museum of Civilization that are identified as Maliseet, (III-E-313 and III-E-319).

Some of these hats may have been worn as smoking caps. Style-conscious men wore formal indoor caps from the sixteenth through the late nineteenth centuries. In the mid-nineteenth century a new, soft form known as a "smoking cap" became all the rage. The shape it took was a cross between the fashionable pillbox and the Turkish fez and they were worn to prevent the hair from smelling of tobacco smoke.

26. Glengarry hat, circa 1820s, 10.5" long x 5.3" wide, decorated in dyed moosehair. The Glengarry bonnet was a hat style adopted by the Scottish Highlanders around 1800. Nineteenth century Hudson Bay Company trade invoices indicate that large quantities of these hats were imported for the Indian trade. The Indians would embellish them with beads, dyed moosehair and ribbon work. The moosehair in this example is sewn onto brown velvet which has a red silk cord trim and a red silk lining. A very similar hat is featured in *Pleasing the Spirits* by Douglas C. Ewing and is identified as Huron, circa 1820.

27. Beaded hat, possibly Iroquois, 1820s-1840s, 8" wide x 5.5" high. An early six paneled hat; the three red panels are on broadcloth, the black is velvet. The beaded border design around the lower band could be a representation of the Iroquois celestial dome and the stylized crown on each panel suggests a Canadian origin.

28. Iroquois hats. The four-paneled hat on the left, 1840s-1850s, 7" wide x 5.3" high is similar to one in the Thaw collection at the Fennimore Art Museum, in Cooperstown, New York, (item #T277) that is identified as Tuscarora.

The six-paneled hat on the right, circa 1850s, 7.5" wide x 6.5" high is decorated in the more classic Iroquois floral style.

28a. A very rare Ruby Ambrotype, mid-1850s, 2.7" x 3.3" of a young man wearing a Glengarry hat. The subjects are identified as William Miller (20 years old) and his sister Mary (18 years old).

Four Glengarry hats, averaging 10" x 5". From left to right:

- Possibly Wabanaki, 1830s - 1840s, glass beads on red broadcloth with blue silk ribbon edge trim.
- Iroquois type, early 1850s, glass beads on black velvet with red cotton edge binding.
- Iroquois type, 1820s - 1840s, glass beads on Navy blue velvet with red silk ribbon edge binding.
- Iroquois type, circa 1850s, glass beads on black velvet with red cotton edge binding.

The tops of these four hats can be seen on the page 1.

29. Stereograph, the Indian Encampment in Saratoga Springs, New York, circa 1870s, 3.4" x 6.9". I have other stereographs of this venue and in some of them the Indians are identified as Oneidas. It's possible that the Mohawk were selling there as well. The scene is not unlike a modern day craft fair.

30. Stereograph, group of Tuscarora women selling their beadwork at Luna Island, Niagara Falls, New York, circa 1860s, 3.4" x 6.9". The American Falls can be seen in the distance.

31. Stereograph, Six Nations Indian Store at Niagara Falls, early 1860s, 3.4" x 6.9". This was above the falls on the American side, looking up the rapids from the bridge on Goat Island.

32a. Little Bear and his mother, St. Regis Mohawks, working on a large pincushion in their New York City apartment, circa 1900.

The following article is from a long defunct, circa 1900 New York City publication called the Metropolitan Magazine. It's a fascinating look into the late nineteenth century life of a Mohawk community that lived in Manhattan and survived by selling their beaded pincushions and other whimsies on the streets of New York.

Lo, The Good Indian of New York.

Lo, the poor Indian, has made his dwelling amid the mighty lodges of the pale-face. With his squaw and pappoose he has taken up the white man's burden of paying rent. For many years there has been an Indian settlement in New York. The colony numbers now, all told, some forty souls. But it is a quiet colony, and few know of the existence of it.

As Lo, of New York, is really a poor Indian, his dwelling place is in the tenement parts of the town. The East Side is too crowded and noisy for him, and so he takes his abode in that portion of the great city, which lies, in and adjacent to old Greenwich Village. Hudson street, King street, and West Broadway are where the Indians of New York live.

They are clannish, or rather they dwell as families together; and it may be stated that, broadly speaking, the Indian colony of New York is one family and its branches. The tribe from which they spring is the Iroquois and they speak that language. They dress, save on special festal occasions among themselves, as the ordinary poorer citizen of New York and his wife.

Meeting the New York Indian or his wife going about their affairs, the average person would think he had chanced upon an Italian man or woman. Originally they were Canadian Indians from St. Regis. Their ancestors were prevailed upon to accompany some showman to New York; the enterprising exhibitor fell a victim to obdurate creditors, and the Indians were thrown upon their own resources.

The head of the family, Chief Dibo – an old man then, and long since deceased – took rooms in a tenement for his family and followers. The women then worked on the bead ornaments, and the men took them out and sold them on the streets. Since then these Indians and their children have dwelt on the island of Manhattan. They still maintain themselves by doing beadwork.

No. 423 West Broadway is where several branches of the Dibo family live. Imagine an old New York home, dormer-windowed, fanlighted, but changed now into a tenement house, and falling into decay from long neglect. Here, in the shadow of the grinding, rattling elevated road, we went up the old-fashioned steps and entered the old-fashioned doorway. The fanlights had long been broken and their sashes above the door were boarded over. This made the hallway dark. But, following our guide, we went up the stairs to the first floor. Here our guide knocked and we were bidden to enter.

Right here a word about our guide. Those who had first told us of New York's Indian colony had also told us that we must have some one with us in the confidence and having the good will of those we sought. This person, our informant said, was James Longfeather, a bright and energetic young Indian, who, by common consent, was looked upon as the present head of the colony. So we sought out Longfeather, and now behold us, with the big chief at our head, knocking at the door of Little Bear.

Inside the room, Little Bear, a stalwart young man of twenty-six, sat at a table near the window. At the other side of the table sat Little Bear's mother, a pleasant-faced woman of forty-odd, and they were making gaily colored, bead-trimmed pincushions. On a chair nearby sat a young man of twenty. A Hebrew peddler, of the type so often exploited in burlesque, stood by the table.

Little Bear was arrayed in trousers and sweater, and his long hair was braided on either side of his forehead. His mother was dressed as an ordinary woman of her age and station in life would be attired. The other young Indian was dressed no different than any other young man you might meet in the neighborhood. He had a derby hat and his overcoat on, and had evidently just come in. He was a pleasant-faced young fellow and spoke excellent English, as did Longfeather and Little Bear. The mother, however, seemed suspicious of the strangers who had crowded in upon her, and only answered briefly in Iroquois the words Longfeather addressed her in the same language.

The young Indian in the derby hat told us that he was a graduate of the Carlisle Indian School and that the woman was his aunt. His name was Louis Dibo, and he was employed by one of the big express companies of New York as a messenger.

The room was scrupulously clean. The floor was carpeted. There was a stove, a neatly made bed with a white counterpane, and there were pictures on the wall. Altogether, it was in no way dissimilar from the tenement home of the average New York workingman. The Hebrew peddler had a bag with him. He filled it with cushions and other articles of New York Indian make, handed money to the makers and departed to dispose of his wares. "He pays them twenty-five and fifty cents apiece for the pin-cushions," said Longfeather, "and he sells them around for thirty-five and seventy-five cents. The Indian men used to sell them, but they were not as smart as the Jews, and it was found that it paid better to let the latter act as middlemen."

Little Bear grinned at this, and both he and his mother kept steadily at work on the objects of Indian art. The pin-cushions were made of bright red and blue flannel, stuffed with excelsior, and then deftly ornamented with beads of various colors. They were the star and heart shaped pin-cushions familiar to the visitor at Niagara Falls and other places where Indian curiosities are sold.

To the question as to whether such things were not often factory made and palmed off as Indian work, both Longfeather and Little Bear answered no, and so did the Carlisle graduate. "I have never seen any of this bogus Indian work," said Longfeather. "I do not believe there is any. But I do know that all Indians make these things and that any of us by looking at them could tell of what tribe the Indians are who worked them."

Mrs. Longfeather (or Frozen Water, which is her tribal name) is a pretty young woman. She is only half Indian, her mother being a French Canadian.

Occasionally a Western Indian, Sioux or Pawnee or Blackfoot, whom Longfeather has foregathered with in the dramatic ventures he makes, stops with his New York brethren for a month or two, but for the main part the New York Indian colony stays to itself, making pin-cushions for the pale-face.

32. Stereograph, Hawley's American Indian Bazaar and observation tower, circa 1870s, 3.4" x 6.9". Located on the Canadian side just over the new suspension bridge, the building was originally built by Phillip Bender. Formally known as Captain Webb's Indian Bazaar, it was later renamed Hawley's. Destroyed by fire sometime after 1883, a hotel was later built on the site. This was one of many places at the Falls where one could purchase Indian souvenirs. A close examination of the detail view reveals that there are posters or paintings depicting Indian scenes between the windows of the building.

33. Daguerreotype, late 1840s, 2.7" x 3.2" of a young couple, perhaps taken on their honeymoon. The woman wears an Iroquois beaded bag that is edged with a beaded fringe and decorated with both floral and double curve motifs. A note on the case of the image reads: "My father and mother Milkins, – Emily Brundage."

34. Carte-de-visite, early 1860s, 2.4" x 4" of a father and son dressed in what appears to be lodge outfits, from a photographer in Albany, New York. The boy is wearing a six-paneled hat, not unlike the one in Figurc 28 and hc also has an Iroquois floral bag at his side. Both are wearing Iroquois beaded moccasins.

35. Daguerreotype of Henrietta and Harry Girer, dated 1852, 2.8" x 3.3". The young girl wears an Iroquois floral bag that has a beaded fringe along the edge. Even at this early date, the floral designs on this bag are already well developed.

36. An engraving of two Indian beadwork vendors in Montreal, from Frank Leslie's Illustrated Newspaper, July 13, 1861, 8" x 9.25". The short article titled *Indian Women of Montreal* that accompanied this illustration follows:

"Who has not seen in the streets of New York, at Saratoga, at Niagara, and especially at Montreal, those short, round, strangely-dressed, half Chinese looking women, whose appearance puzzles foreigners so much, but whom our world unites in terming Indian squaws? Always clad, in the warmest weather, in one vast blue blanket, covering the whole figure from head to foot, always bearing a basket, always quiet, they illustrate, after two centuries of life in contact with white people, the original state of woman among savages – that of uncomplaining, patient endurance. Come upon them in one of their gipsylike encampments, and you will find them at domestic duty, or patiently working their moccasins and baskets; see them abroad, there is still the same animal-like endurance.

Many of these squaws, especially those who have some French blood in their veins, are very beautiful. We have seen one at Niagara who was both sprightly and graceful, and for several years Nancy, at Sharon, was quite a belle, selling her horsehair ear-rings at preposterous prices to young gentlemen. But, as a rule, the half-breed squaw, or the Indian, is a rather plain, somewhat giving to sulking, and seldom very lively; "Ugh!" and "Two shillin'!" forming the average limits of her English conversation.

Our engraving represents two extremely well know moccasin and pincushion sellers of Montreal, who will at once be recognized by such of our readers as are familiar with that city. Like the *florare*, or flower-girls of Florence, they are general acquaintances, but seek their special patrons in strangers. Many of their wares are really beautiful, and are regarded as the most characteristic and charming presents which can be sent from the New World to the Old."

37. Beaded frames, a beaded box and three beaded bags, likely from the Kahnawake Reserve near Montréal, late nineteenth and early twentieth centuries. The large double frame in the foreground is 12" wide x 10.5" high and the one in the upper left corner with the American flags is 9.25" wide x 11.75" high. The one in the center is dated 1926 in beads. It depicts two beavers chewing on a tree.

38.

39.

41.

42.

40.

43.

38. Hand colored carte-de-visite, circa 1870, 2.4" x 4" of a child wearing an Iroquois floral bag. Of the more than two-dozen nineteenth century images I have of people wearing beaded bags, more than half of them are of children.

39. Carte-de-visite, early 1860s, 2.4" x 4" of the famous New York opera star Felitica Vesvali wearing an Iroquois floral bag. Jeremiah Gurney & Sons of New York photographed her for her role as Orsini. From 1855 through 1867, she was a familiar New York City opera star who specialized in singing contralto "trouser roles." After her return to Europe, she left opera for a stage career and often appeared as Hamlet.

40. Ambrotype, mid to late 1850s, 2.7" x 3.2" of a refined young girl proudly wearing her Iroquois floral purse.

41. Carte-de-visite, circa 1860, 2.4" x 4" of a young girl identified as E. E. Marsh, 8 years old. The overall design and bilateral symmetry of her purse suggest a 1850s origin.

42. Ambrotype, mid to late 1850s, 2" x 2.5" of a young girl holding an Iroquois floral bag.

43. Daguerreotype, circa 1850, 2.7" x 3.2" of a well dressed middle aged couple with an Iroquois floral bag.

44. Real photo postcards, circa 1910, 3.5" x 5.5" of Goldie Jamison Conklin, a Seneca of the Heron Clan, from the Allegany Reservation in western New York. Goldie (1891-1974) is wearing a bag of presumably her own manufacture. I have at least a dozen different real photo postcards of her and she is wearing this same bag in all of them. Some of the cards were advertisements for the Cattaraugus Cutlery Co. of Little Valley, New York, advertising their "Indian Brand" knives i.e. the upper and lower right images and the lower left image. She was the subject of my portrait titled "Made of Thunder," see Figure 45.

44a. Top left: real photo postcard of Mary Selmore, Passamaquoddy, 3.5 x 5.5 inches, circa 1906. Top right: cabinet card of Mrs. Marquis, a Kahnawake Mohawk, 4.2 x 6.5 inches, circa 1890. Bottom: real photo postcard, Maime Joseph and her son Russel Joe, Penobscots from Indian Island, circa 1907. These are some of the individuals I've portrayed in my paintings.

45. Title: Made of Thunder. Image size: 22 x 31 inches. Medium: Colored and graphite pencils, acrylic, watercolor and ink. Completed: August 1, 2003. Portrait of Goldie Jamison Conklin, a Seneca. Perhaps the most famous legend in Niagara Falls is that of the Maid of the Mist and the Thunder God Hinum, who the Haudenosaunee believed lived behind the Falls. In one version of this myth, an Indian maiden was sacrificed annually by sending her over the cataract in a canoe, laden with fruit to appease Hinum.

In my portrait of Goldie, I've tried to represent her in a symbiotic relationship with the Falls, a native artist attuned with her surroundings and one proud of her heritage. From her waist belt she wears a beaded bag of her own manufacture. The one that hangs from her neck has a large, central heart motif (top bag in figure 16) that some believe was an early symbol of the Haudenosaunee people.

46. Title: The Basket Maker. Image size: 26.5 x 28.4 inches. Medium: Colored and graphite pencils, acrylic, watercolor and ink. Completed: April 18, 2003. Portrait of Mamie Joseph, a nineteenth century basketmaker from Indian Island, in Old Town, Maine. There is a long tradition of basket making among the Penobscot. While continuing to make utilitarian baskets, late nineteenth century basket weavers began producing forms that were smaller, more portable and highly decorated. Recognizing the Victorian fondness for ornamentation, baskets were embellished with elegant handles, decorative weaves, dyed splints and sweet grass and these forms have become known as "fancy baskets." In this piece I've attempted to capture the indelible spirit of one such artist. Though she is no longer with us, her art survives as a testament to the beauty of the human spirit exemplified by her craft.

47. Title: Penobscot Man. Image size: 25.75 x 35.25 inches. Medium: Colored and graphite pencils, acrylic, watercolor and ink. Completed: December 25, 2004. Portrait of Joe Solomon, a Penobscot. The Solomon's were an old family line from Norridgewock. According to one old Penobscot story, the husband of the "first mother," a mythical female, dragged her dead body across the surface of the Penobscot homeland where her flesh became a corn plant and her bones the tobacco. The great mythological figure Gluskabe told the people to remember her when the smoke of her bones rose before them. From Joe Solomon's traditional Penobscot pipe, a flock of winged spirits carries the essence of the "first mother" back to the spirit world.

48. Title: Teweelema. Image size: 28 x 37 inches. Medium: Colored and graphite pencils, acrylic, watercolor and ink. Completed: February 9, 2006. Malinda Mitchell, best know as Teweelema, was a Wampanoag from the Betty's Neck area of Lakeville, Massachusetts. She was descended from Massasoit, the great sachem of the Wampanoags who greeted the pilgrims in 1620. The Betty's Neck site is today considered sacred by many traditional Wampanoags. In recent times, a large rock, inscribed with an ancient carving of a human hand and foot, was discovered just a few feet from the shore in the waters of Lake Assawampsett. No one knows why the carvings are there but that they are ancient is certain, as the rock has been submerged for many generations. The summer of 2005 was very dry and the lake level dropped enough for the rock and carvings to be exposed, an event that has drawn some of the Wampanoag elders and leaders to the site.

Windsong Blake, the Wampanoag chief of the Assonet band, lives nearby and alerted me to the find. We have walked the grounds there on several occasions and the area has a certain reverence about it. There is something intangible about the place, something you can't quite put your finger on, a presence that can be felt yet is just out of reach. Perhaps it's the spirit of Teweelema and her ancestors walking the grounds of their ancient homeland. This is what I attempted to capture in her portrait.

49. Title: The Story Teller. Image size: 24 x 19.5 inches. Medium: Colored and graphite pencils, acrylic, watercolor and ink. Completed: January 12, 1999. Portrait of Tomah Joseph, (b. 1827 – d. 1914), Passamaquoddy chief, artist and keeper of the creation stories passed down by generations of elders. He is depicted holding a birch bark "Mocuck" created by his own hand. He was a prolific artist and two major themes dominate his work: accounts of Passamaquoddy life and the origin stories. In his art, we often find the words "Mikwid hamin" (Remember me) incised into his bark-work because by remembering something, we keep it alive. In relating these stories we hear the elders speak across the ages. His scenes of Passamaquoddy life depict families in camp, hunting or traveling in canoes or on foot and they dominate the surface of his artwork. The frequency of the owl's appearance in his art suggests that it may have been his personal mark or he may have considered it to be a spirit guide or totem.

Through his craft, he was able to support his family and maintain his cultural identity and in so doing he also helped preserve the collective identity of his people.

50. Title: Dawn of the Red Dove. Image size: 25.75 x 36.5 inches. Medium: Colored and graphite pencils, acrylic, watercolor and ink. Completed: July 7, 2005. Portrait of Mrs. Marquis, a nineteenth century Mohawk from the Kahnawake Reserve near Montreal. The beaded bag she holds in her hand was made by a Kahnawake artist in 1915 and is the same one depicted in Figure 14. The design motifs on her dress and hat are typical of those seen in old photographs of Kahnawake people from the nineteenth century. The Kahnawake Reserve was a Christian mission and the appearance of the dove on many articles of Mohawk clothing may symbolically represents the Holy Spirit, part of the Christian trinity. It's also a symbol of purity and simplicity and may also be a symbolic declaration, in beadwork, that she was a follower of the Christian faith.

51. Title: Dreams of Indian Island. Image size: 22.5 x 35 inches. Medium: Colored and graphite pencils, acrylic, watercolor and ink. Completed: January 12, 2002. Portrait of Molly Molasses, a Penobscot medicine woman of the Bear Clan. Born in the Bangor area around 1775, she died in 1867. Mary Pelagie (or Balassee) Nicola was known to everyone as Molly Molasses. "Molasses" may have been a nickname, as she claimed people called her that "cuz she's sweet" though not everyone agreed with that characterization.
She was known to be a basketmaker and much has been written about the powers she possessed. She had developed a skill or was gifted with the power of healing which she used to help many of her people in their time of need. Some believed that she could cast a hex or spell with just a glance. "If she said you would die," one Indian told Fanny Hardy Eckstorm, "you would die."
In this piece she proudly displays a beaded bag and in so doing proclaims to all that "we are still here!"

52. Title: The White Framed Door. Image size: 26.5 x 29.5 inches. Medium: Colored and graphite pencils, acrylic, watercolor and ink. Completed: October 8, 2003. Portrait of Joe Francis, a Penobscot from Indian Island in Old Town, Maine. Large beaded collars and elaborately beaded cuffs were part of the accoutrements of many notable Penobscots as well as other tribal peoples from the Maritime area. The field of ornamentation on Wabanaki beadwork was of two basic types: the older incorporated the use of the double-curve motif, an ancient design that has many variations. Though its original meaning is lost, I believe it was a graphic representation of the fiddlehead (ostrich fern) that grows abundantly in the Northeast. It was one of the first edible plants to appear in the spring and is high in vitamin A and C. It no doubt had a rejuvenating effect on those who survived the winter on a sparse diet (deficient of ascorbic acid) and as such, it would have been considered a healing or sacred plant. The other form of design augmentation incorporated leaf and floral patterns. These design motifs were all steeped in the mystical worldview of the Northeast woodland people. In this piece, the nearby hummingbird symbolizes the subject's connection to the natural world and the beaded bag and root club he displays denotes two of the many art forms of the Wabanaki people.

53. Title: Red Raven Image size: 24 x 31 inches. Medium: Colored and graphite pencils, acrylic, watercolor and ink. Completed: November 23, 2003. Portrait of Mary Mitchell Selmore, sometimes known as Mollie Mitchell, a Passamaquoddy elder from Pleasant Point and a lifelong basketmaker. She was the wife of Sopiel Selmore, who for many years was both the chief and wampum keeper of the tribe. I struggled with the design of this piece for several weeks and just before I gave up on the idea, I had a dream of a woman standing in a field with numerous red ravens flying about her head. As she walked towards me she was quite composed in their presence and carried herself in perfect harmony with them. They were as much a part of her as she was of them. I don't know if Mary had a special relationship with ravens but this dream became the inspiration for her portrait.